EVERYMAN,
I WILL GO WITH THEE
AND BE THY GUIDE,
IN THY MOST NEED
TO GO BY THY SIDE

HAIKU

❁

SELECTED AND
EDITED BY
PETER WASHINGTON

EVERYMAN'S LIBRARY
POCKET POETS

Alfred A. Knopf New York London Toronto

THIS IS A BORZOI BOOK
PUBLISHED BY ALFRED A. KNOPF

This selection by Peter Washington first published in
Everyman's Library, 2003
Copyright © 2003 by Everyman's Library
Translations from the Japanese are from *Haiku* (4 volumes) by R. H. Blyth,
copyright © 1952 by R. H. Blyth, reprinted by permission of
Hokuseido Press, Japan.

Twelfth printing (US)

A list of acknowledgments to other copyright owners appears at the back
of this volume.

All rights reserved. Published in the United States by Alfred A. Knopf,
a division of Penguin Random House LLC, New York, and in Canada by
Penguin Random House Canada Limited, Toronto. Distributed by Penguin
Random House LLC, New York. Published in the United Kingdom by
Everyman's Library, 50 Albemarle Street, London W1S 4BD and
distributed by Penguin Random House UK, 20 Vauxhall Bridge Road,
London SW1V 2SA.

www.randomhouse.com/everymans
www.everymanslibrary.co.uk

ISBN 978-1-4000-4128-2 (US)
978-1-84159-755-3 (UK)

A CIP catalogue record for this book is available from the British Library

Library of Congress Cataloging-in-Publication Data
Haiku/selected and edited by Peter Washington.
p.   cm.—(Everyman's library pocket poets)
ISBN 978-1-4000-4128-2 (hc: alk paper)
1. Haiku—Translations into English. 2. Haiku. I. Washington, Peter.
II. Series.
PL782.E3H23   2003
895.6′104108–dc21   2003054969

Typography by Peter B. Willberg
Typeset in the UK by AccComputing, North Barrow, Somerset
Printed and bound in Germany by GGP Media GmbH, Pössneck

CONTENTS

FOREWORD

Haiku are epigrammatic nature poems in which the writer aims to achieve maximum effect by minimum means. There is an analogy with Chinese drawings which evoke huge landscapes by a few strokes of the pen. The best haiku are similarly allusive and oblique yet piercingly clear.

Everyone is familiar with the notion that haiku have seventeen syllables, arranged in a pattern of 5-7-5. What matters more is the combination of subtlety, force, economy and technical refinement applied to variations of traditional themes. The trick lies in giving old material a new twist. Despite such sophistication, the form has proved popular. Even today there are said to be more than a million people in Japan writing haiku. The genre has also flourished in Europe and America.

The first and longest section of this volume includes material by the great Japanese masters in pioneering translations by R. H. Blyth. Four dominant figures – Bashō (1644–94), Buson (1715–83), Issa (1763–1827) and Shiki (1856–1902) – define the great age of haiku, but this selection includes items from the fifteenth century to the twentieth.

Haiku emerged from more elaborate poetic forms. Most were written for specific occasions or places familiar to their readers but not to us. Others belong to sequences which sketch a story or a theme. Out of such contexts, haiku can seem merely picturesque unless a cumbersome commentary is supplied. I have tried to avoid this fate by grouping the poems in part one either thematically or within a framework of the seasons to which they are expected to allude.

Although considerable individuality may be discerned in great haiku, personality is traditionally subordinate to themes and techniques. Self-expression may sometimes be the outcome, but the objective is to articulate universal experience in quotidian form.

In an appendix to his magisterial work, Blyth makes the controversial suggestion that the spirit of haiku is present in all great poetry, claiming that there are many haiku 'buried' in familiar English poems. In part two, bearing the notion of universality in mind, I take up this idea, offering some of his examples and more of my own. Leading on from there, the last part of this anthology consists of western haiku and haiku-influenced poems from the twentieth century – a tiny selection from a vast and growing corpus.

PETER WASHINGTON

JAPANESE HAIKU

Translated by R. H. Blyth

BUDDHA NATURE

Plum-blossoms here and there,
It is good to go north,
Good to go south.

BUSON

Simply trust:
Do not also the petals flutter down,
Just like that?

ISSA

When cherry-blossoms are blooming,
Birds have two legs,
Horses four.

ONITSURA

The Great Buddha,
Dozing, dozing,
All the spring day.

SHIKI

Lifting up their horns,
The cattle look at people
On the summer moor.

SEIRA

A spring unseen of men –
On the back of the mirror
A flowering plum-tree.

BASHŌ

14

In the dense mist,
What is being shouted
Between hill and boat?

KITO

The mountain guide
Simply takes no notice
Of the cherry-blossoms.

BUSON

This is all there is;
The path comes to an end
Among the seri.

BUSON

It belongs
Neither to morning nor to evening,
The flower of the melon.

BASHŌ

I heard the unblown flute
In the deep tree-shades
Of the temple of Suma.

BASHŌ

Over the withered moor
The road stretches out
Straight.

BUSON

The puppy that knows not
That autumn has come
Is a Buddha.

ISSA

Visiting the graves –
The old dog
Leads the way.

ISSA

A dog sleeping
At the door of an empty house,
Leaves of the willow-trees scattering.

SHIKI

The cryptomeria, a hundred feet;
The pampas grass,
Six feet.

SHIKI

Has the tail of a horse
The Buddha-nature?
The autumn wind.

SHIKI

One day
Riding on a short-legged horse,
In the haze.

BUSON

A mountain temple;
The sound of the bell struck fumblingly,
Vanishing in the haze.

BUSON

The wind-bells ringing,
While the leeks
Sway.

SHOSEI

Not yet having become a Buddha,
The ancient pine-tree
Idly dreaming.

ISSA

Young leaves come out,
Water is white,
Barley yellowing.

BUSON

My old home:
The face of the snail
Is the face of Buddha.

ISSA

The Buddha on the moor,
From the end of his nose
Hangs an icicle.

ISSA

A swallow
Flew out of the nose
Of the Great Buddha.

ISSA

HAPPINESS

Misty rain;
Today is a happy day,
Although Mt Fuji is unseen.

BASHŌ

This evening . . . the happiness,
While I washed my feet . . .
Those two or three words.

KAITO

The beggar –
He has heaven and earth
For his summer clothes.

KIKAKU

Happiness,
At the white face of the child
In the small mosquito net.

BUSON

In the warmth,
The white house-walls
Ranged along the creek.

SHIKI

Though I have no lover,
I too rejoice:
The change of clothes.

ONITSURA

Asked how old she is,
She holds up the fingers of one hand;
The change of clothes.

ISSA

How lovely,
Through the torn paper window
The Milky Way.

ISSA

PHASES OF
THE MOON

A handle
On the moon –
And what a splendid fan.

SOKAN

The full moon,
Only lovely,
Flawlessly clear.

CHORA

The quarrel
In the ale house,
Revived by the hazy moon.

SHIKI

Moon-gazing:
Looking at it, it clouds over;
Not looking, it becomes clear.

CHORA

All around
That meets the eye
Is cool and fresh.

BASHŌ

The lowing of the cow
In the cow-shed,
Under the hazy moon.

SHIKI

Down the river
The sound of a net thrown; –
A hazy moon.

TAIGI

Carrying a girl
Across the river;
The hazy moon.

SHIKI

The halo of the moon –
Is it not the scent of plum blossoms
Rising up to heaven?

BUSON

Forking
Into the mist,
The stream on the moor.

SHIRAO

Even to the saucepan
Where potatoes are boiling –
A moonlit night.

KYOROKU

Today's moon;
Will there be anyone
Not taking up his pen?

ONITSURA

The thief
Left it behind –
The moon at the window.

                              RYOKAN

Whose is it then,
My children,
This red, red moon?

                              ISSA

The full moon;
My ramshackle hut
Is as you see it.

                              ISSA

The moon has sunk below the horizon:
All that remains,
The four corners of a table.

BASHŌ

The moon in the water;
Broken and broken again,
Still it is there.

CHOSHU

The moon in the water
Turned a somersault
And floated away.

RYOTA

The moon swiftly fleeting,
Branches still holding
The rain-drops.

BASHŌ

The moon of midnight;
A solid mass
Of coolness?

TEISHITSU

The bright moon:
On the tatami
The shadow of the pine-tree.

KIKAKU

37

From time to time
The clouds give rest
To the moon-beholders.

BASHŌ

Autumn's bright moon,
However far I walked, still far off
In an unknown sky.

CHIYO-NI

Scooping up the moon
In the wash-basin,
And spilling it.

RYUHO

Tonight's moon –
Unthinkable
That there was only one.

RYOTA

Mushroom hunting –
Raising my head –
The moon over the peak.

BUSON

One end hanging over
The mountain –
The Milky Way.

SHIKI

BIRDS

Its first note;
The uguisu
Is upside-down.

KIKAKU

The uguisu is singing;
It was yesterday,
At this same hour.

CHORA

Enticed by the distant voice
Of the uguisu,
The sun rises.

CHORA

The uguisu!
Behind the willow,
Before the grove.

BASHŌ

Not being at home,
The uguisu unheard
One whole day.

BUSON

The uguisu, –
Are they brothers?
The same voice!

ISSA

All day long, the voices of the uguisu
Were far off; this day too,
Has drawn to its close.

BUSON

All the long day –
Yet not long enough for the skylark,
Singing, singing.

BASHŌ

The skylark:
Its voice alone fell,
Leaving nothing behind.

AMPU

Voices
Above the white clouds;
Skylarks.

KYOROKU

The skylark
Hides itself
In the expanse of blue sky.

ROKUTO

In the midst of the plain
Sings the skylark,
Free of all things.

BASHŌ

46

The skylark rises,
The skylark falls, –
How green the barley!

ONITSURA

The skylark:
Its voice alone fell,
Itself invisible.

AMPU

Sneezing,
I lost sight
Of the skylark.

YAYU

Their riders sitting sideways,
One horse after another, –
Skylarks in the evening.

ISSA

The voice of the pheasant;
How I longed
For my dead parents.

BASHŌ

As day darkens,
The shooting of a pheasant,
Near the spring mountains.

BUSON

A carpenter
Going to Kameyama;
The cry of the pheasant.

BUSON

In one single cry,
The pheasant has swallowed
The broad field.

YAMEI

A pheasant cries,
As if it had noticed
A mountain.

ISSA

The swallow
Turns a somersault;
What has it forgotten?

OTSUYU

Agitatedly,
The swallow flies out
Of the golden chamber.

BUSON

The sparrow hops
Along the verandah,
With wet feet.

SHIKI

The chirps of the fallen fledgling
Mingle with the chirping
Of the mother-sparrow.

TAIGI

Now making friends,
Now scared of people, –
The baby sparrow.

ONITSURA

Mice in their nest
Squeak in response
To the young sparrows.

BASHŌ

Come and play with me,
Fatherless, motherless
Sparrow.

ISSA

The blind sparrow
Hops on the flower
Of the evening-glory.

GYODAI

The young sparrow
Manifests happiness
In all its wings.

SEKIU

If you are tender to them,
The young sparrows
Will poop on you.

ISSA

Moonlight slants through
The vast bamboo groves:
A hototogisu cries.

BASHŌ

The voice of the hototogisu,
And the five-foot
Irises.

BASHŌ

The cry of a hototogisu
Goes slanting – ah! –
Across the water.

BASHŌ

What! Was it the moon
That cried?
A hototogisu!

BAISHITSU

A carp leaped out,
The water became smooth:
The voice of the hototogisu.

GONSUI

A hototogisu is calling,
But today, just today,
No-one is here.

SHOHAKU

Left behind
By the previous tenant:
The voice of the kankadori.

ISSA

The clouds hasten
To the rhythm
Of the moor-hen's cry.

ISSA

The kingfisher:
In the clear water of the pond
Fishes are deep.

SHIKI

The heron
Is screeching
Under today's moon.

RANSETSU

The water-fowl
Pecks and shivers
The moon on the waves.

ZUIRYU

Low over the rail-road
Wild geese flying:
A moonlit night.

SHIKI

The wild geese –
They ate barley, it is true,
But departing –

YASUI

Under a passage of wild geese,
Over the foot-hills,
A moon is signed.

BUSON

Why should the returning
Wild geese hasten
All through the night?

ROKA

Wild geese returning,
On a night when in every rice-field
The moon is clouding.

BUSON

The wild geese having gone,
The rice-field before the house
Seems far away.

BUSON

Now that the eyes of the hawks
Are darkened in the dusk,
The quails are chirping.

BASHŌ

In the far depths of the forest,
The woodpecker
And the sound of the axe.

BUSON

The woodpecker
Keeps on in the same place:
Day is closing.

ISSA

Birds of passage:
For me too now, my old home
Is but a lodging for the night.

KYORAI

Cleaning a saucepan –
Ripples on the water,
A solitary seagull.

BUSON

The water-fowl
Lays its beak in its breast
And sleeps as it floats.

GINKO

The wren
Earns his living
Noiselessly.

ISSA

The wren is chirruping
But it grows dusk
Just the same.

ISSA

Look! This lonely grave
With the wren
That is always here.

ISSA

61

The wren,
Looking here, looking there –
'Dropped something?'

ISSA

A kite,
In the same place
In yesterday's sky!

BUSON

The sun
In the eye of the falcon
That returned to my hand.

TAIRO

CREATURES

Having slept, the cat gets up,
And with great yawns,
Goes love-making.

ISSA

Loves of the cat;
Forgetful even of the rice
Sticking on his whiskers.

TAIGI

The loves of the cats;
When it was over, the hazy moon
Over the bed-chamber.

BASHŌ

65

How awful!
They have broken the stone wall, –
Cats in love!

SHIKI

The kitten,
Weighed on the balance,
Is still playing.

ISSA

In the winter storm
The cat keeps on
Blinking its eyes.

YASO

The kitten
Holds down the leaf
For a moment.

ISSA

The sound of the bat
Flying in the thicket
Is dark.

SHIKI

The bat
Lives hidden
Under the broken umbrella.

BUSON

The foal
Sticks out his nose
Over the irises.

ISSA

'I make my Appearance,
I, the Toad,
Emerge from My Thicket!'

ISSA

Early dusk:
The mouth of the toad
Exhales the moon.

SHIKI

A snail,
One horn short, one long –
What troubles him?

BUSON

Under the evening moon
The snail
Is stripped to the waist.

ISSA

The snake fleeing away,
The mountain is silent:
This lily flower!

SHIKI

The snake slid away,
But the eyes that stared at me
Remained in the grass.

KYOSHI

In the dawn,
Whales roaring;
A frosty sea.

GYODAI

Mandarin ducks –
A weasel is peeping
At the old pond.

BUSON

70

Foxes playing
Among the narcissus flowers –
A bright moonlit night.

BUSON

The frog
Has both arts –
Of song and of battle.

TEISHITSU

Under the hazy moon,
Water and sky are obscured
By the frog.

BUSON

In the spring, frogs sing;
In summer
They bark.

ONITSURA

The wind falls,
The mountains are clear, –
Now the frogs!

OEMARU

The frog
Looks at me, –
But with a sour face.

ISSA

The frog
Is having a staring-match
With me.

ISSA

The frog rises to the surface
By the strength
Of its non-attachment.

JOSO

When it swims
The frog seems
Helpless.

BUSON

The frog
Riding on the duckweed,
Drifting.

KEISA

Round my hut,
From the first,
The frogs sang of old age.

ISSA

The old pond:
A frog jumps in, –
The sound of water.

BASHŌ

The frog
Enters my gate,
Unawares.

ISSA

On the low-tide beach,
Everything we pick up
Moves.

CHIYO-NI

Ebb-tide;
The crab is suspicious
Of the foot-print.

ROFU

Gazing up
At the end of a great ship
At low tide.

SHIKI

Imitating the human beings,
Pigeons and sparrows
At the ebb-tide.

ISSA

SPRING

Spring begins again;
Upon folly,
Folly returns.

ISSA

Spring begins
Quietly,
From the stork's one pace.

SHOHA

This ramshackle house,
And me just the same as ever –
The first day of spring.

ISSA

Yes, spring has come;
This morning a nameless hill
Is shrouded in mist.

BASHŌ

A day of spring;
In the garden,
Sparrows bathing in the sand.

ONITSURA

A kite
Down on a low tree;
The spring day.

SHIKI

In my hut this spring,
There is nothing,
There is everything.

SODO

A sermon at the cross-roads;
A lot of gibberish,
But this is also spring tranquillity.

ISSA

Emerging a perfect sphere,
And yet how long it is –
The spring day.

SOKAN

Plucking it, plucking it,
Throwing it away, –
The grass of spring.

RAIZAN

The spring day:
A small boat going round
A great vessel.

SHIKI

How heavy
The doors of the Great Gate –
An evening of spring.

BUSON

Spring has come
In all simplicity:
A light yellow sky.

ISSA

The spring day closes,
Lingering
Where there is water.

ISSA

Suddenly thinking of it,
I went out and was sweeping the garden:
A spring evening.

TAIRO

Lighting one candle
With another candle:
An evening of spring.

BUSON

An evening of spring;
Ownerless, it seems,
This abandoned hand-cart.

GYODAI

Treading on the tail
Of the copper pheasant,
The setting sun of spring.

BUSON

A spring evening;
What is the bachelor
Reading?

SHIKI

Sweeping up the fallen leaves
In the train
Of departing Spring.

BUSON

Departing Spring
Hesitates
In the late cherry blossoms.

BUSON

Not lighting the paper lantern,
I grieved
For spring.

KITO

As though this were the lot,
A great deal fell,
Spring snow.

ISSA

In the shallow river,
On hands washing the saucepans,
The spring moon.

ISSA

86

Meeting the messenger on the road,
And opening the letter
The spring breeze.

KITO

The beautiful woman
Jostled by the spring wind,
Her vexation.

GYODAI

On the sandy beach,
Footprints:
Long is the day of spring.

SHIKI

As we grow old,
Even the length of the day
Is a cause of tears.

ISSA

The peacock,
Spreading out his tail
In the spring breeze.

SHIKI

Spring rain:
Everything just grows
More beautiful.

CHIYO-NI

The spring rain:
Between the trees is seen
A path to the sea.

OTSUJI

A stray cat
Asleep on the roof
In the spring rain.

TAIGI

The spring rain;
A little girl teaches
The cat to dance.

ISSA

Spring rain;
A hole in the bed clothes
Where he crept out.

JOSO

Someone is living there;
Smoke leaks through the wall,
In the spring rain.

BUSON

Spring rain:
Rain-drops from the willow,
Petals from the plum tree.

SHOHA

A time of Congratulations:
About average for me –
This is my spring.

ISSA

At night, happiness;
In the day-time, quietness –
Spring rain.

CHORA

The train passes;
How the smoke
Swirls round the young leaves.

SHIKI

When I looked back,
The man who passed
Was lost in the mist.

SHIKI

Will that peach-blossom
Come floating down?
The spring haze.

ISSA

The bell from far away –
How it moves along in its coming
Through the spring haze!

ONITSURA

Spring rain;
An umbrella and a straw coat
Go chatting together.

BUSON

The snow on my hut
Melted away
In a clumsy manner.

ISSA

The snow has melted
On one shoulder
Of the Great Buddha.

SHIKI

Ice and water,
Their differences resolved,
Are friends again.

TEISHITSU

The bottoms of the saucepans
Drying in a row:
The melting of the snow.

ISSA

The snow having melted,
The village
Is full of children.

ISSA

The sun has set;
And the spring water,
Has it increased in volume?

A basket of grass,
And no-one there,
Mountains of spring.

SHIKI

The lights are lit
On the islands far and near:
The spring sea.

SHIKI

The sea of spring,
Rising and falling,
All the day long.

BUSON

The light
On the hoe as it swings up,
The spring moor.

SAMPU

Not knowing
It is a famous place,
A man hoeing the field.

SHIKI

The old man
Hoeing the field,
His hat on crooked.

KITO

Tilling the field;
My house also is seen
As evening falls.

BUSON

Tilling the field:
The man who asked the way
Has disappeared.

BUSON

Tilling the field:
The cloud that never moved
Is gone.

BUSON

One whole day
Tilling the field
In the same place.

SHIKI

A field of rape-flowers:
The sun in the west,
The moon in the east.

BUSON

Sparrows
In the fields of rape,
With flower-viewing faces.

BASHŌ

Flowers of rape;
No whale approaches;
It darkens over the sea.

BUSON

To pluck it is a pity,
To leave it is a pity,
Ah, this violet.

NAOJO

The violet:
Held in the hand,
Yet more lovely.

KOSHU

In the intervals
Of rough wind and rain,
The first cherry-blossoms.

CHORA

The cry of a cock
Is heard too, –
Wild cherry-blossoms.

BONCHO

The morning star,
The cherry-blossoms distinguished
Among the trailing clouds.

KIKAKU

Silent flowers
Speak also
To that obedient ear within.

ONITSURA

Under the cherry-blossoms
None are
Utter strangers.

ISSA

What pains I took,
Hanging the lamp
On the flowering branch.

SHIKI

Cherry-blossoms,
Wet by the clouds
Round the temple bell.

SHIKI

The temple bell dies away.
The scent of flowers in the evening
Is still tolling the bell.

BASHŌ

The pine-tree of Karasaki,
More dim and vague
Than the cherry-blossom.

BASHŌ

What a strange thing,
To be thus alive
Beneath the cherry-blossoms.

ISSA

Evening cherry-blossoms:
Today also now belongs
To the past.

ISSA

103

I came to the cherry-blossoms;
I slept beneath them;
This was my leisure.

BUSON

He sleeps late;
There are his straw sandals,
That trod the fallen petals.

BUSON

The cherry-flowers bloom;
We gaze at them;
They fall, and . . .

ONITSURA

This day on which
The cherry-blossoms fell,
Has drawn to its close.

CHORA

It doesn't seem
Very anxious to bloom,
This plum-tree at the gate.

ISSA

Another blossom of the plum,
And that amount
More warmth.

RANSETSU

The spring scene
Is well-nigh prepared:
The moon and the plum-blossoms.

BASHŌ

Plum-blossoms:
My spring
Is an ecstasy.

ISSA

Suddenly the sun rose,
To the scent of the plum-blossoms,
Along the mountain path.

BASHŌ

How it smells,
The plum-tree next door,
But I cannot see it.

CHORA

The song of the bird!
But the plum-tree in the grove
Is not yet blooming.

ISSA

The flowering branch of the plum
Gives its scent
To him who broke it off.

CHIYO-NI

In the moonlight
The white plum-tree becomes again
A tree of winter.

BUSON

Every night from now
Will dawn
From the white plum-tree.

BUSON

Spreading a straw mat in the field,
I sat and gazed
At the plum-blossoms.

BUSON

The sound of someone
Blowing his nose with his hand;
The plum-blossoms at their best.

BASHŌ

The bat flits and flutters
In the moon
Over the plum-blossoms.

BUSON

The plum-blossoms falling,
Mother of pearl
Is spilt on the table.

BUSON

White plum-blossoms;
In a tea-house of Kitano,
A wrestler.

BUSON

Courtesans
Buying sashes in their room,
Plum-blossoms blooming.

BUSON

White plum-blossoms;
Outside and inside the hedge,
They fall and spill.

CHORA

With every falling petal,
The plum-branches
Grown older.

BUSON

By the old temple,
Peach-blossoms;
A man treading rice.

BASHŌ

Peach-blossoms!
But the ferry-man
Is deaf...

SHIKI

111

A pear-tree in bloom
In the moonlight,
A woman reading a letter.

BUSON

By a house collapsed,
A pear-tree is blooming;
Here a battle was fought.

SHIKI

SUMMER

Summer in the world –
Floating on the waves
Of the lake.

BASHŌ

The melons are so hot,
They have rolled
Out of their leafy hiding.

KYORAI

The melons look cool,
Flecked with mud
From the morning dew.

BASHŌ

Oblivious
Of the gaze of the thief –
Melons in cool.

ISSA

A hoe standing there;
No-one to be seen, –
The heat!

SHIKI

In the fisherman's house
The smell of dried fish
And the heat.

SHIKI

Cold water,
Two biscuits –
Chora's summer.

CHORA

In the market-place,
The smell of something or other –
The summer moon.

BONCHO

This dewdrop world –
It may be a dewdrop,
And yet – and yet –

ISSA

On the lotus leaf
The dew of this world
Is distorted.

ISSA

The dew of the rouge-flower
When it is spilled
Is simply water.

CHIYO-NI

Were it sweet,
It would be *my* dew,
His dew.

ISSA

Never forget
The lonely taste
Of the white dew.

BASHŌ

Coolness
Painted into a picture:
Bamboos of Saga.

BASHŌ

The cool breeze
Fills the empty vault of heaven
With the voice of the pine-tree.

ONITSURA

I sit here
Making the coolness
My dwelling-place.

BASHŌ

The cool breeze:
Crooked and meandering,
It comes to me.

ISSA

You can see the morning breeze
Blowing the hairs
Of the caterpillar.

BUSON

My life, –
How much more of it remains?
The night is brief.

SHIKI

The short night:
In the shallows remains
The crescent moon.

BUSON

Towering clouds
Over a dried marsh
Where a python dwells.

SHIKI

Billowing clouds –
White sails
Crowding in the south.

SHIKI

Billowing clouds –
An ant climbs
On to the ink stone.

SHIKI

Over my legs,
Stretched out at ease,
The billowing clouds.

ISSA

This line of ants,
It continues
From those billowing clouds?

ISSA

The octopus trap:
Fleeting dreams
Under the summer moon.

BASHŌ

How admirable,
He who thinks not, 'Life is fleeting,'
When he sees the lightning flash.

BASHŌ

The summer moon
Is touched by the line
Of the fishing-rod.

CHIYO-NI

The sound of the cracked bell
Is hot too:
The summer moon.

HOKUSHI

Years of my old age;
The summer rains
Falling down the rain-pipe.

BUSON

The legs of the crane
Have become short
In the summer rains.

BASHŌ

The rains of May;
Here is a paper parcel,
Entrusted to me long ago.

SAMPU

Only the staves
Of the pilgrims pass
Across the summer moor.

ISEN

Splashing across the water,
Wiping my feet on the grass, –
The summer moor!

RAIZAN

A horse tied
To a low tree,
In the summer moor.

SHIKI

Was it a flower or a berry
That fell into the water
In the summer grove?

BUSON

126

Entering the summer grove, –
And not a trace
Of him remains.

SHIKI

A clear waterfall;
Into the ripples
Fall green pine-needles.

BASHŌ

Millionaires
Come and drink of this clear water,
And bears.

SHIKI

I take a nap,
Making the mountain water
Pound the rice.

ISSA

Night deepens,
And sleep in the villages;
Sounds of falling water.

BUSON

In the old well
A fish leaps up at a gnat:
The sound of water is dark.

BUSON

A trout leaps;
Clouds are moving
In the bed of the stream.

ONITSURA

A school of trout
Passed by:
The colour of the water.

SHIKI

The quietness:
A chestnut leaf
Sinks through the clear water.

SHOHAKU

The whirligigs,
All pointing their heads
Upstream.

SHIKI

The butterfly having disappeared,
My spirit
Came back to me.

WAFU

O butterfly,
What are you dreaming there,
Fanning your wings?

CHIYO-NI

Butterfly asleep on the stone,
You will be dreaming
Of the sad life of me.

SHIKI

You are the butterfly,
And I the dreaming heart
Of Soshi?

BASHŌ

The fawn
Shakes off the butterfly,
And sleeps again.

ISSA

The butterfly,
Even when pursued,
Never appears in a hurry.

GARAKU

Distracted with the flowers,
Amazed at the moon,
The butterfly.

CHORA

Sheltering with a butterfly
Under the shade of the trees, –
This also is the Karma of a previous life.

ISSA

A fallen flower
Flew back to its branch!
No, it was a butterfly.

MORITAKE

The mosquito smudge
Is also a consolation,
Being alone.

ISSA

Mosquitoes in the day-time;
Buddha hides them
Behind him.

ISSA

A matter for congratulation:
I have been bit
By this year's mosquitoes too.

ISSA

The silver-fish
Are running away, among them
Parents and children.

ISSA

The flea
That is poor at jumping,
All the more charming.

ISSA

My hut is so small,
But please do practise your jumping,
Fleas of mine.

ISSA

Do not kill the fly!
See how it wrings its hands,
Its feet.

ISSA

One human being,
One fly,
In the spacious chamber.

ISSA

The flies at the gate
Raise the sound
Of a fruitful year.

ISSA

The first fire-fly!
It was off, away, –
The wind left in my hand.

ISSA

The fire-fly
Gives light
To its pursuer.

OEMARU

A cage of fire-flies
For the sick child:
Loneliness.

RYOTA

In the river alone
Darkness is slowing, –
The fire-flies.

CHIYO-NI

The willow grown from a cutting;
It has become a night
With fire-flies.

ISSA

Birds were few
And waters distant:
The sound of the cicada.

BUSON

Huge trees are many,
Their names unknown:
The voices of the cicadas.

SHIKI

A cicada is chirping:
The toy wind-mill
Is bright red.

ISSA

The shell of a cicada:
It sang itself
Utterly away.

BASHŌ

The cicada is seen
When it stops crying
And flies.

SHIKI

How piteous:
Beneath the helmet
Chirps a cricket.

BASHŌ

The dragon-flies
Cease their mad flight
As the crescent moon rises.

KIKAKU

The beginning of autumn,
Decided
By the red dragon-fly.

SHIRAO

On the bamboo
That marks the place of a dead man,
A dragon-fly.

KITO

Between the moon coming out
And the sun going in –
The red dragon-flies.

NIKYU

The dragon-fly,
Swift to the distant mountain,
Swift to return.

AKINOBO

Reflected
In the eye of the dragon-fly,
The distant hills.

ISSA

The heavy wagon
Rumbles by:
The peonies quiver.

BUSON

The peony
Made me measure it
With my fan.

ISSA

Having cut the peony,
I felt dejected
That evening.

BUSON

The peonies do not allow
The rain-clouds a hundred leagues round
To approach them.

BUSON

The short night –
The peony opened
During that time.

BUSON

To the candle
The peony
Is as still as death.

KYOROKU

The mountain ant
Stands out clear
On the white peony.

BUSON

An evening orchid –
It hid in its scent,
The flowers white.

BUSON

Among the grasses
A flower blooms white,
Its name unknown.

SHIKI

From what flowering tree
I know not,
But ah, the fragrance!

BASHŌ

A little bit of a nuisance,
These flowers blooming,
The sleeping Buddha.

ISSA

I will knock
At the gate in the darkness,
Where the *u* flowers leave off.

KYORAI

145

Under the hedge, flowers of the *u*:
Do not darken them
With the paper lantern.

HORO

Roses;
The flowers are easy to paint,
The leaves difficult.

SHIKI

The young girl
Blows her nose
In the evening glory.

ISSA

Passing rain,
Drying away
On the convolvulus flower.

SHIKI

The honeysuckle;
With every flower that falls
The voice of the gnats.

BUSON

Ah! Summer grasses!
All that remains
Of the warriors' dreams.

BASHŌ

All the fishermen of the beach
Are away:
The poppies are blooming.

KYORAI

Making his way through the crowd,
In his hand
A poppy.

ISSA

The blossoms have fallen;
Our minds are now
Tranquil.

KOYU-NI

Wistaria flowers;
Resting under them,
A strange couple.

BUSON

Flowers of the wistaria;
Only hanging down their heads
At the parting.

ETSUJIN

Azaleas are blooming;
In this remote mountain village
The boiled rice is white.

BUSON

A woman
Under the azaleas placed in the pot,
Tearing up dried cod.

BASHŌ

The morning-glory too
Can never be
My friend.

BASHŌ

The wild rose growing old,
The pampas grass thinning,
The lespedezas faint and weak.

BUSON

The maiden-flower,
So slender,
Seems the more dewy.

BASHŌ

The maiden-flower
Stands there
Vacantly.

ISSA

Calm days,
The swift years
Forgotten.

TAIGI

Peace and quiet:
Leaning on a stick,
Roaming round the garden.

SHIKI

Peacefulness:
The smoke from Mount Asama;
The mid-day moon.

ISSA

The long day;
My eyes are wearied,
Gazing over the sea.

TAIGI

The slow day;
A pheasant
Settles on the bridge.

BUSON

O snail,
Climb Mt Fuji,
But slowly, slowly!

ISSA

How long the day:
The boat is talking
With the shore.

SHIKI

A willow;
And two or three cows,
Waiting for the boat.

                    SHIKI

A stream
Rowing through the town,
And the willows along it.

                    SHIKI

Into the distance,
The straight line of the canal,
And the willow-trees.

                    SHIKI

The willow-tree
Has forgotten its root
In the young grasses.

BUSON

This willow-tree
That looks like a white cat,
Is also a votive flower.

ISSA

The willow-tree at the gate;
Gazing at it,
Travellers pass on.

CHORA

The puppy asleep,
Pushing his feet
Against the willow-tree.

ISSA

As if nothing had happened,
The crow,
And the willow.

ISSA

You are going away, –
How long the road!
How green the willows.

BUSON

I came back,
Angry and offended;
The willow in the garden.

RYOTA

AUTUMN

Just this morning –
A single paulownia leaf
Has gently fallen.

ISSA

The leaf of the paulownia,
With not a breath of wind,
Falls.

BONCHO

The beginning of autumn;
The sea and fields,
All one same green.

BASHŌ

I go,
Thou stayest:
Two autumns.

BUSON

The autumn wind;
The red flowers
She liked to pluck.

ISSA

The grasses of the garden –
They fall,
And lie as they fall.

RYOKAN

Along this road
Goes no-one
This autumn eve.

BASHŌ

The autumn full moon:
All night long
I paced round the lake.

BASHŌ

The autumn of my life;
The moon is a flawless moon,
Nevertheless –

ISSA

In travelling attire,
A stork in late autumn rain:
The old master Bashō.

CHORA

Ah, grief and sadness!
The fishing-line trembles
In the autumn breeze.

BUSON

The beginning of autumn:
A lamp from some-one's house is seen;
It is not quite dark.

BUSON

It is seen
In the papier-mâché cat,
This morning of autumn.

BASHŌ

This autumn,
How old I am getting:
Ah, the clouds, the birds!

BASHŌ

To the sound of the flute
The waves also approach;
Suma in autumn.

BUSON

Deep autumn:
My neighbour –
How does he live?

BASHŌ

Autumn evening;
A crow perched
On a withered bough.

BASHŌ

The wind of autumn
Blew first of all
Upon the morning-glories.

CHORA

An autumn evening;
Without a cry
A crow passes.

KISHU

An autumn eve:
There is a joy too
In loneliness.

BUSON

The flying leaves
In the field at the front
Are enticing the cat.

ISSA

Blowing from the west
Fallen leaves gather
In the east.

BUSON

Leaves falling,
Lie on one another –
The rain beats on the rain.

GYODAI

The young child –
But when he laughed –
An autumn evening.

ISSA

The long night;
The monkey thinks how
To catch hold of the moon.

SHIKI

The long night;
The sound of water
Says what I think.

GOCHIKU

The stream hides itself
In the grasses
Of departing autumn.

SHIRAO

Bent over by the rain,
The ears of barley
Make it a narrow path.

JOSO

Even so, even so,
Submission before Yonder –
The end of the year.

ISSA

The scissors hesitate
Before the white chrysanthemums,
A moment.

BUSON

They spoke no word,
The host, the guest,
And the white chrysanthemum.

RYOTA

My eyes, having seen all,
Came back to
The white chrysanthemums.

ISSHO

That is what happens:
Recovering from illness,
The chrysanthemums smell cold.

OTSUJI

Every year
Thinking of the chrysanthemums,
Being thought of by them.

SHIKI

Chrysanthemum flowers;
And wafted along also,
The smell of urine.

ISSA

The yellow chrysanthemums
Lose their colour
In the light of the hand-lantern.

BUSON

At the bend of the road,
The temple in sight –
Wild chrysanthemums.

SHIKI

Write me down
As one who loved poetry
And persimmons.

SHIKI

Examining
Three thousand haiku:
Two persimmons.

SHIKI

Wild persimmons,
The mother eating
The bitter parts.

ISSA

A hundred different gourds
From the mind
Of one vine.

CHIYO-NI

The hanging bridge:
Creeping vines
Entwine our life.

BASHŌ

A chestnut falls:
The insects cease their crying
Among the grasses.

BASHŌ

What a huge one, how splendid it was –
The chestnut.
I couldn't get at it.

ISSA

In the dark forest
A berry drops:
The sound of water.

SHIKI

175

A bird sang,
Knocking down
A red berry.

SHIKI

Peeling a pear,
Sweet drops trickle down
The knife.

SHIKI

Even before His Majesty,
The scarecrow does not remove
His plaited hat.

DANSUI

It walked with me
As I walked,
The scarecrow in the distance.

SANIN

Frost at midnight:
I would sleep, borrowing
The sleeves of the scarecrow.

BASHŌ

The bright full moon –
As if it were nothing special,
The scarecrow standing there.

ISSA

177

The owner of the field
Goes to see how the scarecrow is,
And comes back.

BUSON

In this fleeting world
The scarecrow also
Has eyes and nose.

SHIKI

The sparrows are flying
From scarecrow
To scarecrow.

SAZANAMI

Going out of the house
Ten paces –
And the vast autumn sea.

SHIKI

The water run off
Becomes the darkness
Of each field.

BUSON

WINTER

The first frost;
Fine morning weather –
How the rice-water tastes.

CHORA

A red berry
Spilled
On the hoar-frost of the garden.

SHIKI

The first snow –
The leaves of the daffodils
Are just bending.

BASHŌ

In the winter river,
Pulled up and thrown away –
A red turnip.

BUSON

Among the winter trees
When the axe sank in –
How taken aback I was at the scent.

BUSON

The previous owner:
I know it all –
Down to the very cold he felt.

ISSA

The light in the next room also
Goes out;
The night is chill.

SHIKI

Resigned to death by exposure,
How the wind
Cuts through me.

BASHŌ

First winter rain:
The monkey also seems
To want a small straw cloak.

BASHŌ

A poor lodging:
The whimpering of the dog
In the rain at night.

BASHŌ

A winter night;
Without any reason,
I listen to my neighbour.

KIKAKU

The leeks
Newly washed white –
How cold it is.

BASHŌ

The sound
Of a rat on a plate –
How cold it is.

BUSON

Night –
Biting the frozen brush
With a remaining tooth.

BUSON

After killing the spider,
A lonely
Cold night.

SHIKI

My bones
Feel the quilts –
A frosty night.

BUSON

A winter evening:
The needle has disappeared –
How dreadful.

BAISHITSU

As one of us,
The cat is seated here –
The parting year.

ISSA

Walking in the night –
Snow is falling,
A farewell to the year.

SHARA

I intended
Never to grow old,
But the temple bell sounds.

JOKUN

The crescent moon
Is warped and bent –
Keen is the cold.

ISSA

You light the fire;
I'll show you something nice, –
A great ball of snow!

BASHŌ

I could eat it!
This snow that falls
So softly, so softly.

ISSA

A shower came;
Running inside,
It cleared up.

YUINE

I walk over it alone
In the cold moonlight –
The sound of the bridge.

TAIGI

The shadow of the trees;
My shadow is moving
In the winter moonlight.

SHIKI

Not a single stone
To throw at the dog –
The winter moon.

TAIGI

A stray cat
Running off under the eaves –
The winter moon.

JOSO

In the icy moonlight
Small stones
Crunch underfoot.

BUSON

A moonlit night:
The sticks of the wicker fish-trap –
Their shadows are uneven.

SHIRAO

Colder even than snow,
The winter moon
On white hairs.

                    JOSO

At the voice of the copper pheasant
That cannot sleep,
The moon is chill.

                    KIKAKU

The gale will not let
The cold winter rain
Fall to the ground.

                    KYORAI

Rain begins to fall:
The thatcher turns
And looks at the sea.

JOSO

The stars on the pond –
Again the winter shower
Ruffles the water.

SORA

Winter rain
Falls on the cow-shed;
A cock crows.

BASHŌ

On an umbrella, a patter of raindrops,
But it enters next door –
The evening darkens.

RANRAN

The first frost
Fine morning weather –
How the rice-water tastes.

CHORA

The old pond –
A straw sandal sunk to the bottom,
Sleet falling.

BUSON

The first snow of the year
On the bridge
They are making.

BASHŌ

The first snow –
Beyond the sea
What mountains are they?

SHIKI

While the fowls
Were asleep –
A heavy fall of snow.

KIEN

We gaze
Even at horses,
This morn of snow.

BASHŌ

One long line of river
Winds across
The snowy moor.

BONCHO

On moor and mountain
Nothing stirs,
This morn of snow.

CHIYO-NI

The straight hole
Made by pissing
In the snow outside the door.

ISSA

The snow we saw come down –
Has it fallen
This year too?

BASHŌ

The windy snow
Falling and blowing around me
As I stand here.

CHORA

Should I perish
On this snowy moor, I also
Shall become a snow-Buddha.

CHOSUI

Many umbrellas
Are passing by
This eve of snow.

HOKUSHI

An umbrella – one alone –
Passes by:
An evening of snow.

YAHA

A bulbul cried,
And cried no more:
Snow fell through the dusk.

ARO

The mountain blast!
The hail is driven
Into the horse's ear.

TAIRO

On the deck
The sound of the hail
Is dark.

SHIKI

I woke up suddenly,
With the ice of a night
When the water-pot burst.

BASHŌ

A rat approaches
The freezing oil
Of the lamp.

BUSON

The winter river –
Not enough water
For four or five ducks.

SHIKI

Winter seclusion –
Listening, that evening,
To the rain in the mountain.

ISSA

Winter seclusion –
On the gold screen
The pine-tree ages.

BASHŌ

Mountains seen also
By my father, like this,
In his winter confinement.

ISSA

The flame is motionless,
A rounded sphere
Of winter seclusion.

YAHA

Winter seclusion:
Once again I will lean against
This post.

BASHŌ

Putting in the water,
The vase received
The camellia.

ONITSURU

A camellia flower fell;
A cock crew;
Another fell.

BAISHITSU

A camellia –
It fell in the darkness
Of an old well.

BUSON

One fell, –
Two fell, –
Camellias.

SHIKI

The flower of the camellia-tree
Fell,
Spilling its water.

BASHŌ

The camellia flower
Was going to fall,
But it caught in its leaves.

SHOHA

All the evening the only sound,
The falling
Of the white camellia flowers.

RANKO

205

Up in the well-bucket
Of the dawn of day, –
A camellia.

KAKEI

NEW YEAR

NEW YEAR

This New Year's Day
That has come at last –
It is just a day.

HORO

New Year's Day;
The hut just as it is,
Nothing to ask for.

NANSHI

New Year's Day:
What I feel, has been too much
For the words.

DAIO

A day of light
Begins to shine
From on the heads of the pilchards.

BUSON

That is good, this too is good –
New Year's Day
In my old age.

ROYTO

The first day of the year:
I remember
A lonely autumn evening.

BASHŌ

210

New Year's Day;
The desk and bits of paper –
Just as last year.

MATSUO

The first day of the year;
Through the door of my hut,
A field of barley.

SHOHA

The stream through the fields –
Ah, the sound of the water!
It is New Year's Day.

RAIZAN

Planting my stick
In the quagmire,
The first sun of the year.

ISSA

New Year's Day:
What luck! What luck!
A pale blue sky!

ISSA

New Year's Day;
I do not hate
Those who trample on the snow.

YAYU

New Year's presents;
The baby in the bosom also
Holds out her tiny hands.

ISSA

In my hands a branch of plum-blossoms,
Spoke the greetings
Of the New Year.

SHIKI

The smoke
Is now making
The first sky of the year.

ISSA

The first dream of the year;
I kept it a secret
And smiled to myself.

SHO-U

The Great Morning:
Winds of long ago
Blow through the pine-tree.

ONITSURA

WESTERN HAIKU

WESTERN LANE

TRADITIONAL

The sun shines warm,
And the babe leaps up
On his mother's arm.

WORDSWORTH

The lark's shrill fife
May come
From the fallow.

SCOTT

The lark now leaves her wat'ry nest,
And climbing,
Shakes her dewy wings.

DAVENANT

As a dare-gale skylark
Scanted in a dull cage
Man's mounting spirit in his bone-house.

HOPKINS

In the broad daylight
Thou art unseen,
But yet I hear thy shrill delight.

SHELLEY

A young beech tree
On the edge of the forest
Stands still in the evening.

ALDINGTON

Two trees
Like swans' necks
Twine in the garden

SWENSON

Only the beak-leaved boughs
Dragonish
Damask the tool-smooth bleak light...

HOPKINS

A lonely pool,
And let a tree
Sigh with her bosom over me.

DAVIES

Loveliest of trees,
The cherry now is hung with bloom
Along the bough.

HOUSMAN

I will touch
A hundred flowers
And pick not one.

MILLAY

The pliant harebell
Swinging in the breeze
On some gray rock.

WORDSWORTH

Daffodils,
With the green world
They live in.

KEATS

The yellow wall-flower
Stained
With iron brown.

THOMSON

With excellent precision
The tulip bed
Inside the iron fence . . .

WILLIAMS

Unloved, the sun-flower,
Shining fair,
Ray round with flames her disc of seed . . .

TENNYSON

Whither,
O splendid ship,
Thy white sails crowding?

BRIDGES

We passed in silence,
And the lake
Was left without a name.

E. G. SCOTT

The blue noon is over us,
And the multitudinous billows
Murmur at our feet.

SHELLEY

As kingfishers catch fire
Dragonflies
Draw flame.

HOPKINS

Annihilating all that's made
To a green thought
In a green shade.

MARVELL

Over his own sweet voice
The stock-dove
Broods.

WORDSWORTH

The meadows
Were drinking at their leisure;
The frogs sat meditating.

THOREAU

Far in the stillness,
A cat
Languishes loudly.

WHITMAN

A violet
By a mossy stone,
Half hidden from the eye.

WORDSWORTH

Every leaf and every flower
Pearled
With the self-same shower.

KEATS

The moon doth with delight
Look round her
When the heavens are bare.

WORDSWORTH

227

The innocent moon
That nothing does
But shine.

F. THOMPSON

The moonlight steeped
In silentness
The steady weathercock.

COLERIDGE

By the sea,
Under the yellow
And sagging moon.

WHITMAN

The long day wanes;
The slow moon climbs;
The deep moans round with many voices.

TENNYSON

Over the old wooden bridge
No traveller
Crossed.

THOREAU

The railroad bridge
Is a sad song
In de air.

LANGSTON HUGHES

The frozen wind
Crept on above,
The freezing stream below.

SHELLEY

Ivy serpentine
With its dark buds and leaves,
Wandering astray.

WORDSWORTH

In shades the orange bright,
Like golden lamps
In a green night.

MARVELL

MODERN

TS'AI CHI'H

The petals fall in the fountain,
The orange-coloured rose-leaves,
Their ochre clings to the stone.

POUND

IN A STATION OF THE METRO

The apparition of these faces in the crowd;
Petals on a wet, black bough.

POUND

ALBA

As cool as the pale wet leaves
                    Of lily-of-the-valley
She lay beside me in the dawn.

POUND

Little moths reel shudderingly out of the beech;
they will die this evening and never know
that it was not Spring.

RILKE

LINES

Leaves are grey green,
the glass broken, bright green.

WILLIAMS

From JANUARY MORNING

IV

– and the sun, dipping into the avenues
streaking the tops of
the irregular red houselets,
                              and
the gray shadows dropping and dropping.

XII

Long yellow rushes bending
above the white snow patches;
purple and gold ribbon
of the distant wood:
        what an angle
you make with each other as
you lie there in contemplation.

WILLIAMS

PRELUDE TO WINTER

The moth under the eaves
with wings like
the bark of a tree, lies
symmetrically still –

And love is a curious
soft-winged thing
unmoving under the eaves
when the leaves fall.

WILLIAMS

THE HURRICANE

The tree lay down
on the garage roof
and stretched, You
have your heaven,
it said, go to it.

WILLIAMS

From PATERSON

When I saw
the flowers

I was
thunderstruck!

You should not
have been –
Tulips, she said
and smiled.

WILLIAMS

In my medicine cabinet,
The winter fly
Has died of old age.

KEROUAC

Birds singing
In the dark
– Rainy dawn.

KEROUAC

Evening coming –
The office girl
Unloosing her scarf.

KEROUAC

Arms folded
To the moon,
Among the cows.

KEROUAC

Missing a kick
At the icebox door
It closed anyway.

KEROUAC

FOR BERKELEY

City of buds and flowers
Where are your fruits?
Where are your roots?

SNYDER

ON CLIMBING THE SIERRA
MOUNTAINS AGAIN

Range after range of mountains
Year after year after year.
I am still in love.

SNYDER

first snow –
the spider is evicted
from my boot

FORRESTER

temple ruins –
pieces of a Buddha
still praying

FORRESTER

239

end of autumn –
finding myself
in a field of thistle

FORRESTER

writing a haiku
in the sand …
a wave finishes it

FORRESTER

summer evening …
fanning myself
with a paper moon

FORRESTER

winter afternoon –
a crow blackens
the white sky

FORRESTER

lily:
out of the water . . .
out of itself

VIRGILIO

heat before the storm:
a fly disturbs the quiet
of the empty store

VIRGILIO

New Year's Eve:
pay phone receiver
dangling

VIRGILIO

the cathedral bell
is shaking a few snowflakes
from the morning air

VIRGILIO

Easter morning...
the sermon is taking the shape
of her neighbour's hat

VIRGILIO

lone red-winged blackbird
riding a reed in high tide –
billowing clouds

VIRGILIO

the autumn wind
has torn the telegram and more
from my mother's hand

VIRGILIO

the hinge of the year:
holding up candles in church
lighting up our breaths

VIRGILIO

autumn twilight:
the wreath on the door
lifts in the wind

VIRGILIO

Time after time
caterpillar climbs this broken stem,
then probes beyond.

HACKETT

Half of the minnows
within this sunlit shallow
are not really there.

HACKETT

244

A bitter morning:
sparrows sitting together
without any necks.

HACKETT

looking deeper
and deeper into it
the great beech

WILLS

a marsh hawk
tips the solitary
pine

WILLS

245

laurel in bloom
she lingers awhile
at the mirror

WILLS

deep winter . . .
all day long the mountainside
in shadow

WILLS

a box of nails
on the shelf of the shed
the cold

WILLS

the swan's head
turns away from sunset
to his dark side

VIRGIL

Quiet afternoon:
water shadows
on the pine bark.

VIRGIL

rustling beneath
the leaf cover, I pluck
the bean cool

VIRGIL

247

holding you
in me still...
sparrow songs

VIRGIL

a phoebe's cry...
the blue shadow
on the dinner plates

VIRGIL

not seeing
the room is white
until that red apple

VIRGIL

Cliff dweller ruins
And the silence of swallows
Encircling silence.

JEWELL

This evening stillness . . .
Just the ruined cowbell
Found by the pasture gate.

JEWELL

Shooting the rapids!
– a glimpse of a meadow
gold with buttercups

SPIESS

A light river wind;
on the crannied cliff
hang harebell and fern

SPIESS

Patches of snow
mirrored in the floating stream;
a long wedge of geese

SPIESS

A long wedge of geese;
straw-gold needles of the larch
on the flowing stream

SPIESS

Winter moon;
a beaver lodge in the marsh,
mounded with snow

SPIESS

Winter wind –
bit by bit the swallow's nest
crumbles in the barn

SPIESS

ACKNOWLEDGMENTS

The publishers would very much like to thank the Hokuseido Press for permission to reprint a substantial number of poems from *Haiku* (4 volumes) by R. H. Blyth, copyright © 1952 by R. H. Blyth.

Thanks are also due to the following copyright holders for their permission to reprint:

FORRESTER, STANFORD: 'first snow', 'temple ruins', 'end of autumn', 'writing a haiku', 'summer evening' and 'winter afternoon' by Stanford Forrester, copyright © 2003. Reprinted by permission of the author. HACKETT, JAMES W.: 'Time after time', 'Half of the minnows' and 'A bitter morning' by James W. Hackett from *The Zen Haiku and Other Zen Poems of J. W. Hackett*, Japan Publications, Inc., © 1983 by James W. Hackett. Reprinted by permission of Haiku Distributors, nirvana@maui-net, Maui, Hawaii (USA). JEWELL, FOSTER: 'This evening stillness' by Foster Jewell, from *Passing Moments*, Sangre de Cristo Press, copyright © 1974, and 'Cliff dweller ruins' by Foster Jewell, from *Haiku Sketches*, Sangre de Cristo Press, copyright © 1971. Reprinted by permission of Deborah LaFauce (granddaughter). KEROUAC, JACK: 'In my medicine cabinet', 'Birds singing', 'Straining at the padlock', 'Evening coming', 'Arms folded' and 'Missing a kick' by Jack Kerouac, from *Scattered Poems* by Jack

Gurga. VIRGIL, ANITA: 'rustling beneath' and 'holding you' by Anita Virgil, from *One Potato Two Potato Etc*, Peaks Press, copyright © 1991 by Anita Virgil, and 'the swan's head', 'quiet afternoon', 'a phoebe's cry…' and 'not seeing' by Anita Virgil, from *A 2nd Flake*, copyright © 1974 by Anita Virgil. Reprinted by permission of the author. VIRGILIO, NICHOLAS: 'lily', 'heat before the storm', 'New Year's Eve', 'the cathedral bell', 'Easter morning…', 'lone red-winged blackbird', 'the autumn wind', 'the hinge of the year' and 'autumn twilight' by Nicholas Virgilio, from *Selected Haiku*, co-published by Burnt Lake Press and Black Moss Press, copyright © 1988 Nicholas A. Virgilio. Reprinted by permission of Anthony Virgilio. WILLIAMS, WILLIAM CARLOS: 'January Morning' (Sections IV and XII), 'Lines' and 'Paterson' (8-line excerpt) by William Carlos Williams, from *Collected Poems: 1909–1939*, Volume I, copyright © 1938 by New Directions Corp and Carcanet Press. Reprinted by permission of New Directions Publishing Corp and Carcanet Press. 'The Hurricane' and 'Prelude to Winter' by William Carlos Williams, from *Collected Poems 1939–1962*, Volume II, copyright © 1944 by New Directions Publishing Corp and Carcanet Press. Reprinted by permission of New Directions Publishing Corp and Carcanet Press. WILLS, JOHN: 'looking deeper', 'a marsh hawk', 'laurel in bloom' and 'a box of nails' by John Wills, from *Reed Shadows*, Black Moss Press and

255